Barnyard Animals

Goats on a Farm

Abbie Mercer

PowerKiDS press

New York

For the Swedish goat

Published in 2010 by The Rosen Publishing Group, Inc.
29 East 21st Street, New York, NY 10010

First Edition

Editor: Amelie von Zumbusch
Book Design: Kate Laczynski
Photo Researcher: Jessica Gerweck

Photo Credits: Cover, pp. 1, 5, 9, 11, 13, 15, 19, 21, 23, 24 (beard, horns, kid) Shutterstock.com; p. 7 © www.istockphoto.com/Lilli Day; p. 17, 24 (balance) © www.istockphoto.com/Anton Ferreira.

Library of Congress Cataloging-in-Publication Data

Mercer, Abbie.
  Goats on a farm / Abbie Mercer. — 1st ed.
     p. cm. — (Barnyard animals)
  Includes index.
  ISBN 978-1-4042-8049-6 (library binding) — ISBN 978-1-4042-8056-4 (pbk.)
ISBN 978-1-4042-8060-1 (6-pack)
  1. Goats—Juvenile literature. 2. Domestic animals—Juvenile literature. I. Title. II. Series.
  SF383.35.M47 2010
  636.3'9—dc22
                          2008047336

Manufactured in the United States of America

Contents

Have you ever seen a goat? Goats are playful and interesting animals.

Goats live on farms. People have raised goats for thousands of years.

There are many kinds of goats. Some goats are white, while others are black or brown.

Most goats have **horns**. Many kinds of goats have **beards**.

11

Goats eat plants, such as grass. Goats also often eat hay, or dried grasses.

Goats are smart animals. They are interested in the world around them.

Goats are very good climbers. They have excellent **balance**.

Baby goats are called **kids**. Kids drink their mothers' milk.

Goat kids like to play. They run and jump.

Farmers often raise goats for their milk. People also keep goats as pets.

Words to Know

balance

beard

horns

kid

Index

Web Sites

Due to the changing nature of Internet links, PowerKids Press has developed an online list of Web sites related to the subject of this book. This site is updated regularly. Please use this link to access the list:
www.powerkidslinks.com/byard/goats/